Lerner SPORTS

# ANNIKA SÖRENSTAM
## LPGA CHAMPION

T0015715

ABBE L. STARR

LERNER PUBLICATIONS ◆ MINNEAPOLIS

SPORTS THRILLS *MEET* RESEARCH SKILLS

Lerner SPORTS

Free Database Trial: **lernersports.com**

Lerner Publications Company
An imprint of Lerner Publishing Group, Inc.
241 First Avenue North
Minneapolis, MN 55401 USA

For reading levels and more information, look up this title at www.lernerbooks.com.

Main body text set in Myriad Pro Semibold.
Typeface provided by Adobe.

**Editor:** Lauren Foley

**Library of Congress Cataloging-in-Publication Data**

Names: Starr, Abbe L., author.
Title: Annika Sörenstam : LPGA champion / Abbe L. Starr.
Description: Minneapolis, MN : Lerner Publications , [2023] | Series: Epic Sports Bios (Lerner Sports) | Includes bibliographical references and index. | Audience: Ages 7–11 years | Audience: Grades 2–3 | Summary: "Pro golfer Annika Sörenstam took the LPGA Tour by storm during her career. Learn about her life, records and awards, and more in this exciting bio"— Provided by publisher.
Identifiers: LCCN 2022008708 (print) | LCCN 2022008709 (ebook) | ISBN 9781728476490 (Library Binding) | ISBN 9781728478531 (Paperback) | ISBN 9781728482422 (eBook)
Subjects: LCSH: Sorenstam, Annika, 1970- —Juvenile literature. | Women golfers—Sweden—Biography—Juvenile literature. | Golfers—Sweden—Biography—Juvenile literature.
Classification: LCC GV964.S63 S73 2023  (print) | LCC GV964.S63  (ebook) | DDC 796.352092 [B]—dc23/eng/20220314

LC record available at https://lccn.loc.gov/2022008708
LC ebook record available at https://lccn.loc.gov/2022008709

Manufactured in the United States of America
1-52230-50670-6/7/2022

# TABLE OF CONTENTS

# A CHAMPION

Tucked in the Rocky Mountains of Colorado Springs, Colorado, Annika Sörenstam nervously watched and wondered whether her dreams of winning the 1995 US Women's Open would come true. The golf course was difficult with narrow fairways and fast greens. Sörenstam

Sörenstam watches the ball fly at the 1995 US Women's Open.

# FACTS AT A GLANCE

**Date of birth:** October 9, 1970

**Position:** pro golfer

**League:** Ladies Professional Golf Association (LPGA)

**Professional highlights:** was Rolex Player of the Year eight times; won six Vare Trophies; is the only woman to shoot a 59 in an LPGA tournament

**Personal highlights:** played on the Swedish National Team; played tennis as a kid; created the ANNIKA Foundation in 2007

started strong with a 67 in the first round, and by the second, she was in the lead!

During the third round, Sörenstam missed the greens and putted poorly. When knocked off the leaderboard, she stayed calm and said, "One thing I had learned is always to play as if you've got a chance to win." Sörenstam was five strokes behind Meg Mallon.

Sörenstam avoided mistakes. But one of Mallon's shots went into a pond during the last round. It was Sörenstam's chance to catch up! By the eighth hole, Sörenstam tied with Mallon for the lead. Then Sörenstam made three

Sörenstam putts her ball toward the hole.

Sörenstam showing off the 1995 US Women's Open trophy

birdies, pulling ahead. Even though Sörenstam accidentally hit balls into sand traps and missed a few putts, she still held the lead by one stroke.

Everyone watched Mallon approach the final hole. Would she sink a 20-foot (6 m) putt to force a playoff round? Sörenstam held her breath as Mallon's ball rolled closer and closer to the hole. It finally stopped 1 foot (0.3 m) short of the cup. Sörenstam won!

# A DREAM TO WIN

**A**nnika Sörenstam was born on October 9, 1970, in Bro, Sweden. Bro is a city near Stockholm, Sweden's capital. But even before she was born, Annika was around golf. Her mother, Gunilla Sörenstam, played while she was pregnant with Annika.

Annika's mother worked at a bank. Annika's father, Tom Sörenstam, worked at the technology company IBM. Annika

A church in Bro, Sweden, the town where Sörenstam was born

has one younger sister, Charlotta. Annika's family loved sports. At a very young age, Annika learned to ski, golf, and play tennis.

At the age of five, Annika began attending tennis summer camps. She played for seven years and was one of the top 10 players of her age group by the age of 10. But Annika wanted to be the best. When she was 12, she gave up tennis and tried golf. She practiced every day. As Annika improved, she hoped to become a professional player. Her father told her, "You know, Annika, there are no shortcuts to success."

## A SHY WINNER

When she was young, Annika was very shy. She would purposely miss putts so she wouldn't win and have to give a victory speech. Her coaches made a rule that both the runner-up and winner had to talk. Annika thought if she had to give a speech, she might as well win!

Sörenstam waves to the crowd with her putter in 2006. Her hard work paid off.

Annika knew that to be the best golfer, she would have to work harder than everyone else. She worked on her golf swing. She also practiced with the Swedish Golf Federation, which helped strengthen her body and mind. In 1987, at 16, Annika joined the Swedish National Team.

At 20, Sörenstam accepted a scholarship to the University of Arizona in Tucson. The desert was a perfect place to play golf. After moving to the US, Sörenstam had culture shock—to feel unsure or confused in a new and different place or culture. She struggled to remember English words, the coaching was different, and she had a strict schedule. None of this would stop Annika from winning.

Sörenstam attended college in Tucson, Arizona

# DETERMINED TO SUCCEED

In her first year of college, Sörenstam was 21 and already a strong player. She finished in the top 10 in all but one event. She won the 1991 National Collegiate Athletic Association (NCAA) Women's Golf Championship. She was named an All-American as one of the best college golfers in the nation. And she was named the NCAA Co-Player of the Year.

Sörenstam concentrates as she tees off.

Sörenstam taking a powerful shot

In 1992, Sörenstam came in second place to Vicki Goetze while defending her NCAA title. They met again at the US Women's Amateur event. On the last hole, Sörenstam and Goetze were tied. Sörenstam tried to clear a pond but missed. She lost the tournament by one shot. Even though she didn't win, she knew that she was a strong player and decided to leave college to become a professional golfer.

That summer, Sörenstam played in the US Women's Open as an amateur. She tried not to be scared by the talented golfers around her. She struggled with putting and tied for 63rd out of 66 golfers. She had a lot of work to do to improve.

## NOTING HER FEELINGS

Sörenstam tracked her feelings on a notepad. When she was feeling happy, strong, and focused, she recorded it. When she felt frustrated, she checked her notepad to remember how she felt when she played well. This helped her stay calm while playing golf.

Sörenstam lining up a shot in 1994

Sörenstam needed to earn her LPGA Tour card to play in tournaments. She earned her card by the 1994 season. In her first two tournaments, she missed the cut to compete. This motivated her to try even harder. Sometimes she played well, and other times she struggled. But she never quit.

Sörenstam's game improved. In 1994, she tied for second in the Women's British Open. She was named Rookie of the Year. But Sörenstam wanted to win an LPGA championship.

# CHAMPION AT LAST

Sörenstam got her wish at the 1995 US Women's Open when she was 24. It was her first major championship win. When presented with the trophy, she was so happy she could barely speak. All she could say was "Thank You." She wasn't ready for the fame that followed. When she trained for competitions, she had to brace herself for the attention that came with being a champion.

Sörenstam proudly holds up her 1995 US Women's Open trophy.

Laura Davies smashes a shot from a sand trap.

Sörenstam faced Laura Davies in the 1995 Samsung World Championship of Women's Golf. They fought for the lead by playing an extra hole. Sörenstam chipped in the ball from 45 feet (14 m) away for the win. Then she became the year's top money winner on the LPGA Tour.

That year, Sörenstam earned many awards in the US and Sweden. In the US, she was named the Rolex Player of the Year. She also won the Vare Trophy, awarded to the player with the lowest scoring average. Sweden named her their Athlete of the Year.

In 1996, Sörenstam's success continued with a record win at the US Women's Open. "I entered that magical zone where every shot goes where you want it to go," she said. During her last round, Sörenstam birdied two holes. On one of the holes, her first shot even hit the pin, or the pole that marks the hole. She also sank a 20-foot (6.1 m) putt for an eagle. She ended with eight under par and a US Women's Open record-setting score of 272.

Sörenstam zeroes in on a putt. Her good aim has helped her win many events.

Sörenstam made history in 1998. She broke a scoring record of 19 under par in the Japan Airlines Big Apple Classic. And at eight strokes fewer than the next best player, she broke the tournament record for biggest lead.

She earned her third Player of the Year and third Vare Trophy and made LPGA history with a season scoring average below 70. As if her 1998 success wasn't enough, Sörenstam made history again in 1999 at the Sara Lee Classic with a lowest-ever first-round score of 61.

Sörenstam stays focused while competing.

Despite all her success, Sörenstam still wanted to win another major event. She devoted an extra hour every day to practicing putting, and she hired a personal trainer. She ran, swam, biked, kickboxed, and did more than 700 sit-ups a day. She was in the best shape of her life.

# LEGENDARY WINS

In 2001, Sörenstam returned to one of her college courses in Phoenix, Arizona, for the Standard Register Ping tournament. She couldn't be stopped. Her putts were cool and collected. In her first 13 holes, she made 12 birdies. Sörenstam broke a record during that match, becoming the first woman to score a 59 in a professional round.

Sörenstam crouches down to line up a shot.

In 2002, Sörenstam shattered her own 1998 LPGA record with a season average of 68.7. By the start of the 2003 season, she had made more money than anyone else in LPGA history. That year, she was invited to compete in a Professional Golfers Association (PGA) tournament and a skins game. In a skins game, players compete for a prize on every hole. She was the first woman to play on the PGA Tour since 1945. Then she won the 2003 Women's British Open. With that victory, she had won every major tournament at least once and earned a career grand slam.

Sörenstam grins and holds up the 2003 Women's British Open trophy.

Sörenstam chips a ball into the air in 2003.

Sörenstam joined the World Golf Hall of Fame in 2003. In 2005, she became the first LPGA player with three straight wins in the same major. She also won her eighth Rolex Player of the Year award and sixth Vare Trophy, more than any LPGA player before her.

Her wins continued in 2006. In a playoff round of the US Women's Open, Sörenstam won by four strokes. It had been 10 years since her last Open victory. The hard-fought win was especially sweet. But she had more to celebrate that year. From 2000–2006, she never finished an event outside of the top 20.

Sörenstam has fun while she golfs.

In 2007, Sörenstam started the ANNIKA Foundation. Part of the ANNIKA business brand, the foundation offers golf opportunities to girls of all ages and abilities worldwide. It also promotes active lifestyles in young people.

Sörenstam focused on her foundation in 2007. But she still took time to golf.

Sörenstam with Mike McGee and their children

Sörenstam retired in 2008. But she still had wins to celebrate. She married her husband, Mike McGee, the following year. Sörenstam and McGee had a daughter, Ava, in 2009. They also had a son, Will, in 2011.

Sörenstam continues to have an impact on the golf world. In 2021, with her family by her side, she won the US Senior Women's Open by eight strokes. She led the tournament wire to wire—she was in the lead for all rounds of play. That year, she received the Presidential Medal of Freedom and became the first woman president of the International Golf Federation.

Sörenstam tees off at the US Senior Women's Open. Her powerful shots and leading score showed she was still a golf champion.

Sörenstam poses at a 2021 LPGA event. She still takes time to support the tour.

At the end of the year, Sörenstam focused on her family and ANNIKA. But she hoped to play in the 2022 US Women's Open. No matter what comes next, Sörenstam knows the commitments and sacrifice it takes to be on top. "Success isn't only about the goal you choose," she said, "It's about the experience, the effort, and the journey."

# SIGNIFICANT STATS

Won eight Rolex Player of the Year awards (1995, 1997–1998, 2001–2005)

Won six LPGA Vare Trophies (1995–1996, 1998, 2001–2002, 2005)

Was the first woman to score a 59 in a pro match

In 1998, became the first LPGA player to have a season average below 70

In 2002, broke her season average record and had a career low average of 68.7

# GLOSSARY

**amateur:** an athlete who is not paid for competing in a sport

**birdie:** one stroke less than par

**chip:** a shot from near the green that lofts the ball to roll on the green

**eagle:** two strokes less than par

**fairway:** the short-cut grass between the tee and the green

**green:** the very short-cut grass surrounding the hole

**par:** the number of strokes a golfer should expect to need to get the ball from the tee into the cup

**professional:** an athlete who earns money by competing in a sport

**putt:** to take a shot on a green to try to hit the ball into the hole

**scholarship:** money awarded to a student to help pay for school

# SOURCE NOTES

6    Annika Sörenstam, *Golf Annika's Way*, with the editors of *Golf Magazine* (New York: Gotham Books, 2004), 14.

9    Bill Pennington, "My Swings with Annika," *New York Times*, April 12, 2009, https://www.nytimes.com/2009/04/13/sports/golf /13pennington.html.

16   Sörenstam, *Golf Annika's Way*, 15.

18   Sörenstam, 18.

27   Sörenstam, XV.

# LEARN MORE

ANNIKA Foundation
https://www.annikafoundation.org

Annika Sörenstam
https://www.lpga.com/players/annika-sorenstam/81956/overview

Fishman, Jon M. *Golf's G.O.A.T.: Jack Nicklaus, Tiger Woods, and More.* Minneapolis: Lerner Publications, 2022.

Mattern, Joanne. *12 Reasons to Love Golf.* Mankato, MN: 12-Story Library, 2021.

*Sports Illustrated Kids:* Golf
https://www.sikids.com/tag/golf

Wells, Don. *Golf.* New York: AV2 by Weigl, 2020.

# INDEX

# PHOTO ACKNOWLEDGMENTS

Image credits: J.D. Cuban/Allsport/Getty Images, pp. 4, 6, 16; Keattikorn/Shutterstock, p. 5; AP Photo/Ed Andrieski, p. 7; Zejo/Wikimedia Commons (Public Domain), p. 8; AP Photo/Reed Saxon, pp. 10, 23; Sean Pavone/Shutterstock, p. 11; Sport Picture Library/Alamy Stock Photo, p. 12; liewig christian/Getty Images, p. 13; Steve Munday/ALLSPORT/Getty Images, p. 15; Sheldon/Popperfoto/Getty Images, p. 17; PONTUS LUNDAHL/TT News Agency/AFP/Getty Images, p. 18; Scott Halleran/ALLSPORT/Getty Images, pp. 19, 20; Warren Little/Getty Images, p. 21; Nick Laham/Getty Images, p. 22; AP Photo/Matt Dunham, p. 24; Tony Marshall/Getty Images, p. 25; Rich Schultz/Getty Images, p. 26; Michael Reaves/Getty Images, p. 27; Keattikorn/Shutterstock, p. 28.

Cover: AP Photo/Craig Lassig; AP Photo/Gail Burton.